Beginner's Guide to
Silk Painting

For
Jenny, Ben
and Jack

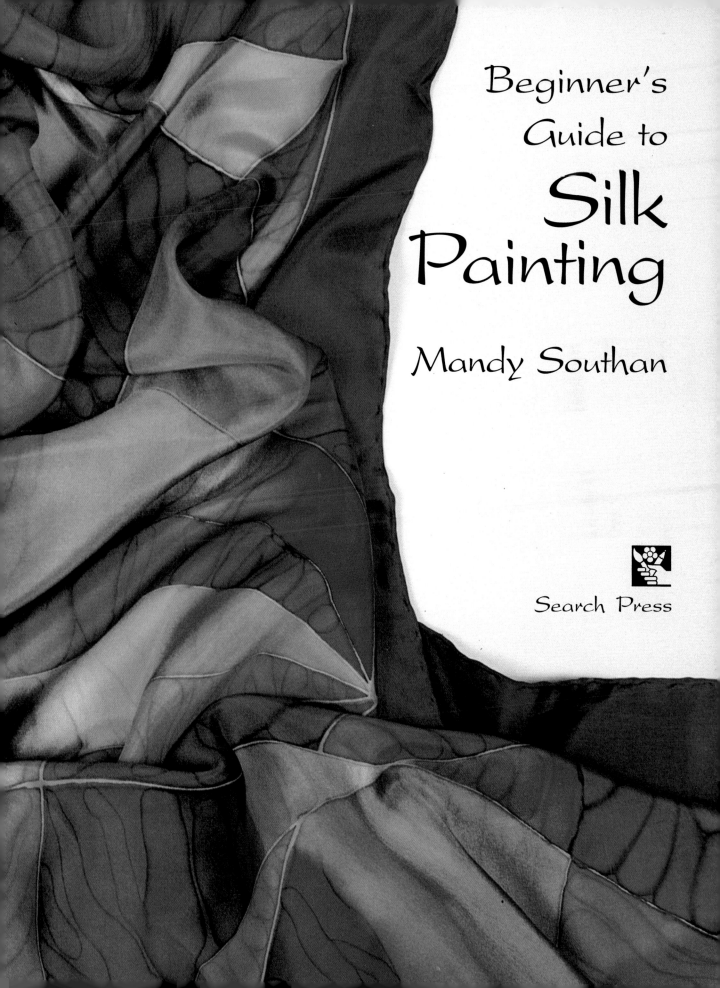

Beginner's Guide to Silk Painting

Mandy Southan

Search Press

First published in Great Britain 1997

Search Press Limited
Wellwood, North Farm Road,
Tunbridge Wells, Kent TN2 3DR

Reprinted 1998, 1999

ISBN 0 85532 802 9

Suppliers
If you have any difficulty in obtaining any of the
materials and equipment mentioned in this book,
then please write for a current list of stockists,
including firms who operate a mail-order service, to
the Publishers.
Search Press Limited, Wellwood,
North Farm Road, Tunbridge Wells,
Kent TN2 3DR, England

Publishers' note
It is the publishers' custom to recommend synthetic
materials as substitutes for animal products
wherever possible. However, for the purposes of
painting with wax, synthetic fibres will melt and so
natural fibres are given as the only viable
alternative. Please note that for most other
purposes, brushes made from artificial fibres are just
as satisfactory as those made from natural fibres.

Printed in Spain by Elkar S. Coop. Bilbao 48012

*Firstly, I would like to thank my family and espe-
cially my husband, Ian, for his continual support
and encouragement, my sister Jill, and my mother,
who first taught me how to see, appreciate and
paint. I would also like to thank my editors,
Chantal Porter and Roz Dace, Julie Wood and
everyone else at Search Press who helped produce
this book and made the experience of working on it
so interesting and enjoyable. Lastly, I would like to
thank Sue Benn who taught me how to teach, and
my many students from whom I have learnt so
much and who have enriched my life considerably.*

Page 1

Singapore Orchids

*This colourful picture uses steam-fix dyes on silk habotai.
The resist lines around the flowers and stems are applied
with turquoise and green dye-tinted gutta plus, and the
background is patterned by overpainting with
brushstrokes of diffusing medium and weak violet dye.
The flowers are carefully shaded by blending darker
shades into lighter areas. A variation of this picture
appears on page 52.*

55 x 76cm (21$^1/_2$ x 30in)

Contents

INTRODUCTION . 6

Basic materials 8

USING COLOUR 12

Colour mixing 14
COLOUR WHEEL

Sunflower scarf 18
PAINTING ON DAMP SILK

Mandarin cushion 22
PAINTING ON DRY SILK

Textured effects 24
USING SALT

USING RESISTS 26

Iris picture 28
USING GUTTA

Fossil scarf 32
USING OUTLINER

Autumn leaves 36
USING GUTTA WITH A BLENDED WASH

Sea spray scarf 38
USING WAX

Kingfisher cushion 42
USING WAX

MOVING ON 46

Velvet cushion 48
USING DISCHARGE PASTE

Striped scarf 50
USING DIFFUSING MEDIUM

Exotic orchid wallhanging 52
USING DYE-TINTED GUTTA

Greek mountain landscape 54
USING SALT SOLUTION

Flower and grape panel 56
USING ANTI-SPREAD

Finishing off 57
ADDING DETAIL

GLOSSARY 58

Common mistakes 63

INDEX 64

INTRODUCTION

It is difficult to describe what it is that makes painting on silk so fascinating and compulsive. It has a magical quality which attracts people, and they usually love it from the first time they try it. The richness and vibrancy of the colours, combined with the shimmering lustre of the silk, means that even the simplest idea can be transformed into something special and unique. It is a relaxing and absorbing process, making it the perfect foil for the stress of modern life.

You do not have to know how to draw or paint to produce beautiful work, and pleasing results can be achieved in a short time. By just applying colours on to wet or dry silk, you can produce wonderful abstract shapes or realistic pictures. There are also many striking linear patterns which can be adapted and traced on to silk to produce stunning designs. If you do make a 'mistake' when you are working, improvise, be creative and adapt the design.

The projects are intended to introduce you to basic silk painting skills and provide a starting point from which you can develop your own ideas. The techniques shown are easy to learn and if you have never tried silk painting before, you will find that you soon have the confidence to paint your own pictures.

Before you begin working through a project, it is worth spending a little time preparing for it. You may find it helpful to collect together all the materials listed at the beginning of the project and to read through the text. All the projects in this book can be painted using either dyes or paints unless otherwise specified. The results, however, will differ, so it is always a good idea to practise, test colours and experiment on cheap silk before embarking on the projects using more expensive silks. It is never possible to exactly replicate a silk painting because of the nature of the paints and dyes, and the fact that each type of silk will take the paint in a slightly different way – because of this, some of the finished items in this book differ slightly from those shown in the step-by-step demonstrations.

Silk painting frees inhibitions and helps to develop self-confidence in artistic expression. I am sure you will be amazed at how quickly you can learn to express your individuality and creativity using the wide range of silk painting materials that are available today.

Basic materials

Silk painting is not expensive. You can start with a few colours, a good brush and a small piece of light-weight silk. Materials can be added as your skills and interest develop. A list of materials required accompanies each project, but in addition you will need jars of clean water, paper towelling, scissors, palettes and droppers.

Please note that inside frame measurements are given for each project. Do not worry if you have not got the exact size frame, as measurements are intended as a guide only. For each project, remember to cut your silk a little bigger than the specified inside frame measurement to allow for pinning up.

The items listed here are shown on pages 10–11.

1. Silks   Various types of silk are suitable for painting on, including silk habotai, crepe de chine, crepe georgette and gauze chiffon.

2. Scissors   These are used for cutting the silk.

3. Sponge   This is used for damping the silk, and sponging on resists, discharge paste or wax.

4. Droppers   These are used for transferring paints and dyes from their bottles to a palette.

5. Palettes   These are used for mixing colours in. The ones with deep wells are most useful. Plastic palettes will stain with silk paints; porcelain palettes are more expensive but will not stain.

6. Gutta bottle with gutta nib   This is used for applying resists in a fine line.

7. Clear gutta   This is used as a resist.

8. Metallic and coloured outliner   These are used as resists.

9. Gutta and outliner   These are used as resists. Many are supplied in jars, but they can be transferred into gutta bottles. Gutta plus can be coloured with steam-fix dyes.

10. Soft pencil (3B) and autofade marker   These are used for drawing on the silk.

11. Brushes   Round watercolour brushes with good points are used for paints and dyes; old natural-haired brushes are used for wax; 2.5cm and 5cm (1in and 2in) foam brushes are used for painting large areas of silk.

12. Thickener   This is also known as *epaississant*. It is used to thicken paint and dye to prevent it from spreading.

13. Steam-fix silk dyes   These are used for painting on the silk.

14. Diffusing medium   This is also known as thinner or *diluant*. It is used with steam-fix dyes.

15. Anti-spread medium for dyes   This is also known as *anti-fusant* or primer. It is used with steam-fix dyes to stop the colours spreading.

16. Iron-fix silk paints   These are used for painting on the silk.

17. Anti-spread medium for paints   This is also known as *malgrund*. It is used with iron-fix paints to prevent the colours from spreading.

18. Jam jars   You will need at least two jars filled with water: one for rinsing brushes in and one for mixing and diluting colours.

19. Hairdryer   This is used to speed up the drying of resists, paints and dyes.

20. Iron   This is used to iron-fix silk paints, and to remove wax from silk.

21. Salt   Fine and coarse-grained salt is used to create random patterns on damp, painted silk. It can also be mixed with water to make a salt solution which treats the silk prior to painting.

22. Three-point silk pins These are used to pin the silk to the frame.

23. Stenter pins These are used to pin awkward shapes of silk and silk with pre-rolled edges to the frame.

24. Wooden frame This is used for stretching the silk.

25. Wax granules Batik wax granules are ideal for use as a resist in silk painting.

26. Tjantings These are used to apply hot wax.

27. Electric wax pot This is used to melt the wax; it should be thermostatically controlled for safety. You could use a double saucepan with water in the base instead.

28. Bamboo steamer, cotton cloth, string and tinfoil circles This equipment is needed for steam-fixing silk dyes.

29. Paper towelling This can be dabbed directly on to the silk to remove excess water or colour, and brushes can be dabbed on to it for the same reason.

30. Rubber gloves It is advisable to wear protective gloves when working with dyes as they can stain hands.

31. Apron It is advisable to wear an apron when working with dyes or paints to protect clothes from staining.

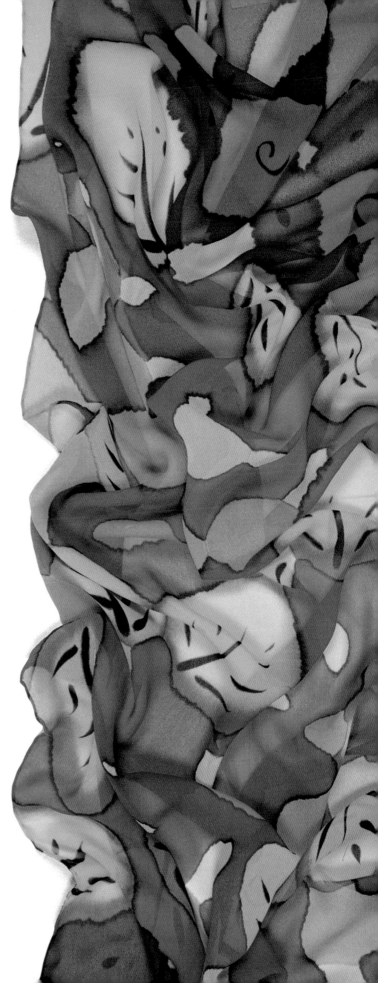

Basic materials

These are the basic materials required for silk painting. You may find it useful to refer to the glossary on pages 58–62 which contains additional information about many of the materials that are shown here.

1. Silks

2. Scissors

3. Sponge

4. Droppers

5. Palettes

6. Gutta bottle and gutta nib

7. Clear gutta

8. Metallic and coloured outliners

9. Gutta and outliner

10. Pencil and autofade marker

11. Brushes

12. Thickener

13. Steam-fix dyes

14. Diffusing medium

15. Anti-spread medium for dyes

29. Paper towelling

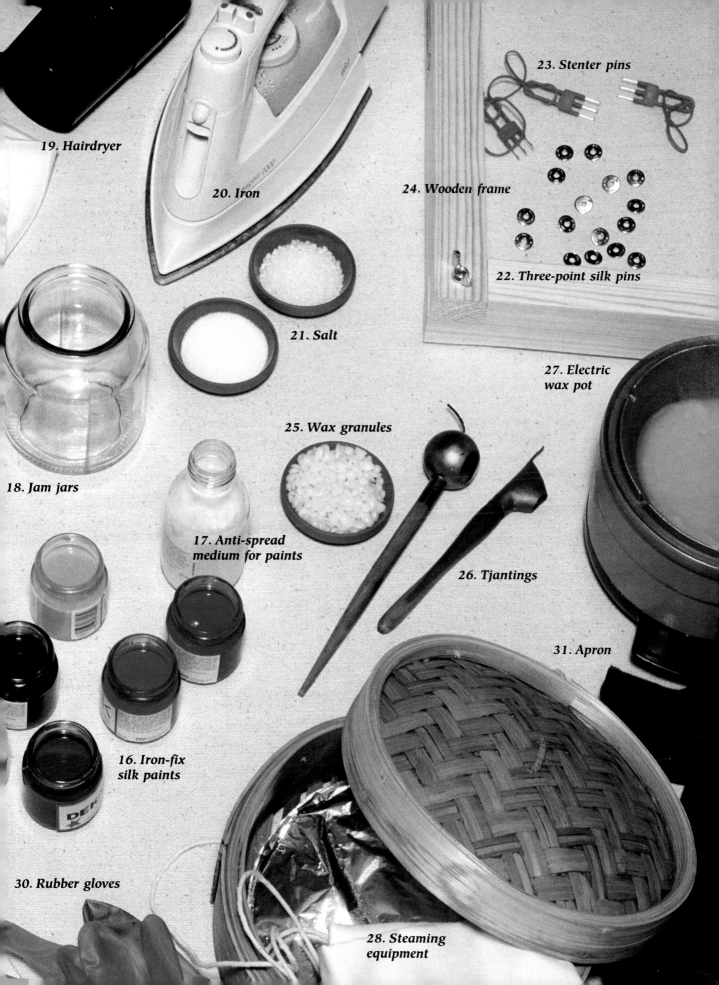

19. Hairdryer

20. Iron

23. Stenter pins

24. Wooden frame

22. Three-point silk pins

21. Salt

27. Electric wax pot

25. Wax granules

18. Jam jars

17. Anti-spread medium for paints

26. Tjantings

31. Apron

16. Iron-fix silk paints

30. Rubber gloves

28. Steaming equipment

USING COLOUR

The special colorants for painting on silk fall into two main categories: iron-fix silk paints and steam-fix silk dyes. Fixing the colours makes the painted silk colourfast and washable.

When you apply paints or dyes for the first time, it is surprising to discover how the colours spread and blend of their own accord. Many different effects can be achieved by blending, layering and overpainting colours. Use a large brush which will hold plenty of colour to apply the paint or dye. Paint the colour evenly across the area, always keeping the spreading edge damp to avoid watermarks. A brush with a good point will allow you to paint intricate parts.

Paints blended into damp silk

Paint diluted with water

Paints used on dry silk and overpainted on dry colours

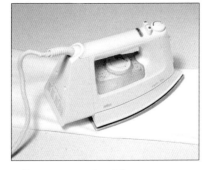

Silk paints are fixed by ironing (see page 58).

Paints used on damp silk

Paint dried quickly with a hairdryer

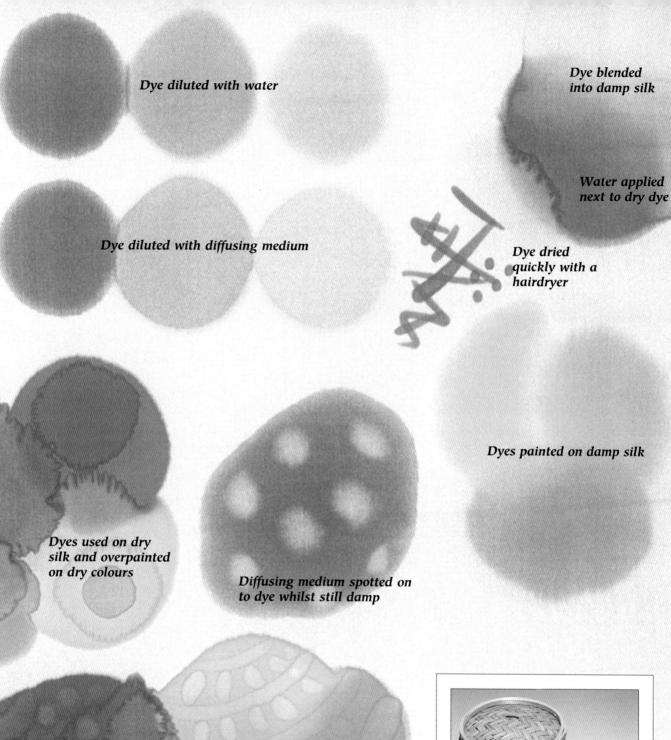

Dye diluted with water

Dye blended into damp silk

Dye diluted with diffusing medium

Water applied next to dry dye

Dye dried quickly with a hairdryer

Dyes painted on damp silk

Dyes used on dry silk and overpainted on dry colours

Diffusing medium spotted on to dye whilst still damp

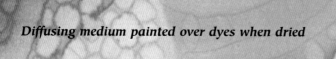

Diffusing medium painted over dyes when dried

Silk dyes are fixed by steaming (see pages 58–59).

13

Colour mixing

Silk paints and dyes are supplied in a large range of colours; it is often difficult to know which colours to choose and how many to select to make a good basic range. In fact, only six colours are necessary and from these you can mix a vast range of colours. By combining two or three of the following colours in different proportions, and by adding water to produce tints, almost any colour imaginable can be mixed. Good colour mixing comes with practice, so find time to experiment and build up your own colour chart.

All the projects in this book list only the basic blues, reds and yellows needed, and from these you will need to mix up the other colours. Of course, you can vary the colours and tones if you wish, and experiment with your own colour schemes.

Two reds
orangey red (vermilion)
violety red (fuchsia or magenta)

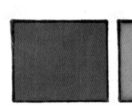

Two blues
violety blue (ultramarine)
greeny blue (cyan or cerulean)

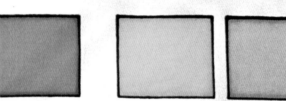

Two yellows
greeny yellow (lemon)
orangey yellow (golden)

Greens

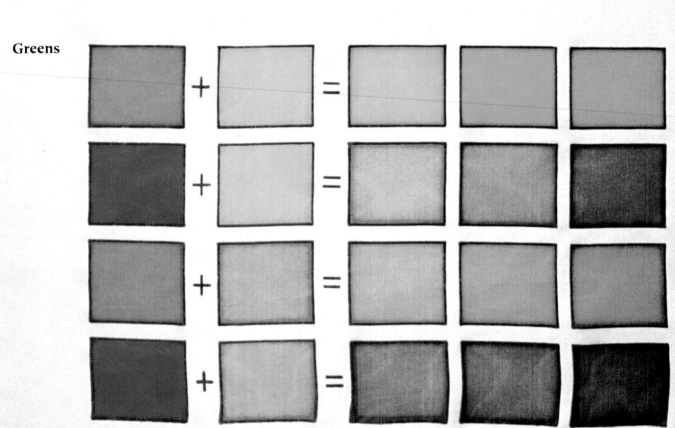

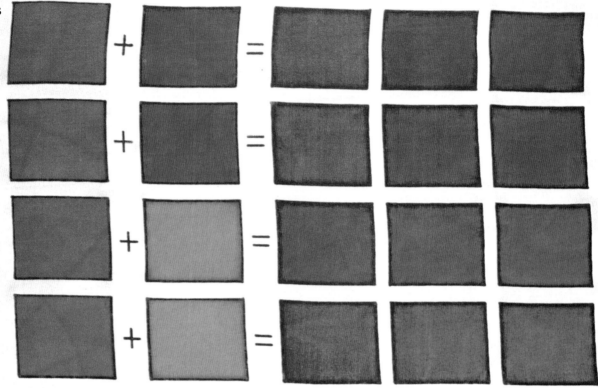

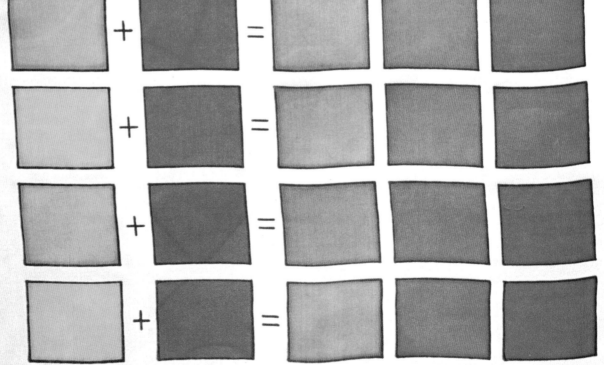

COLOUR WHEEL

The colour wheel shows the six basic colours with three mixed colours between each pair, arranged in the sequence of the spectrum. Each colour has been diluted twice to show tints; the more water or diffusing medium you add, the lighter the colour becomes.

A colour wheel is a useful way of identifying complementary colours, which lie opposite each other on the colour wheel: yellows and violets, reds and greens, oranges and blues. When complementaries are mixed together, wonderful browns, greys and neutral colours result, e.g. red mixed with green will produce brown. Altering the proportions of red and green will produce different browns.

Complementary colours also visually enhance each other. Use complementary pairs in your paintings to create exciting effects: yellows against violets, reds against greens, and oranges against blues. Blend small amounts of one into the other to reduce the intensity of the colour, e.g. a small amount of orange added to blue will darken the blue.

More unified and harmonious paintings tend to be achieved by working with a small palette of colours. Try to work with a maximum of three basic colours (one red, one blue and one yellow) mixed and blended in lots of different ways.

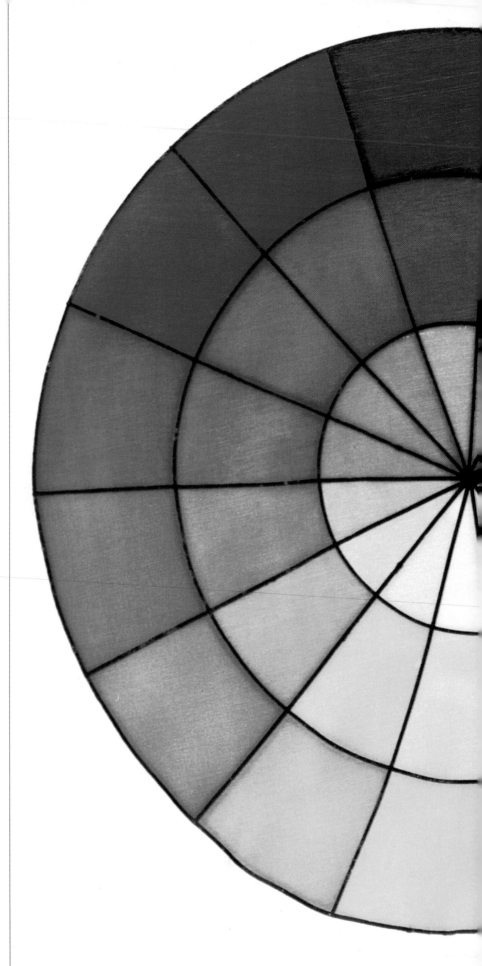

16

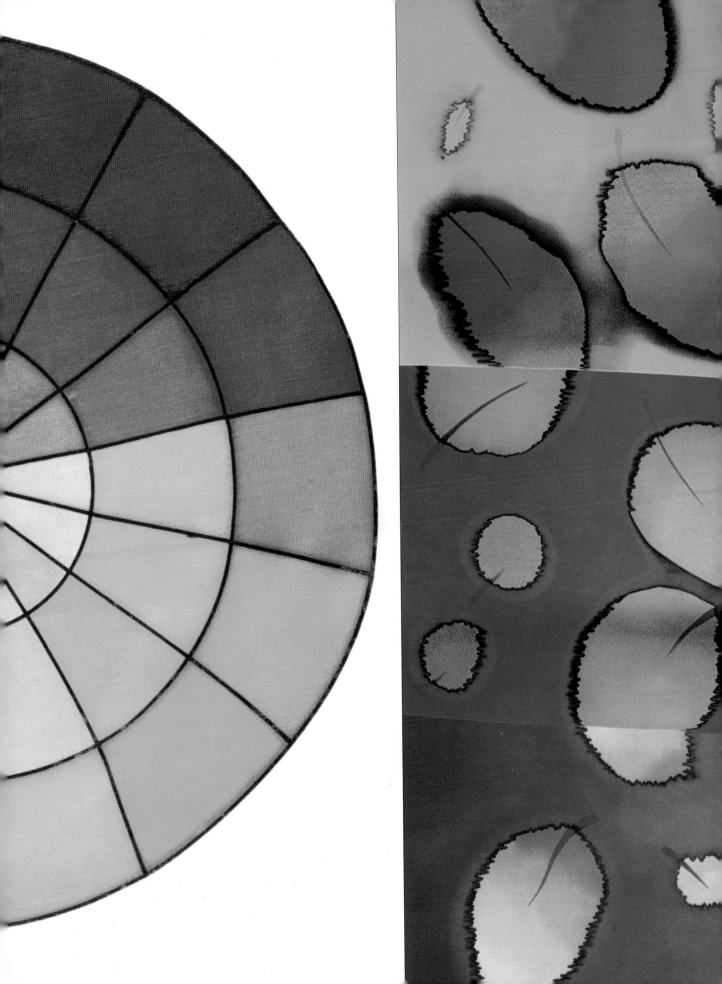

Sunflower scarf

PAINTING ON DAMP SILK

When colours are painted on to damp silk, they merge and dry with soft, blurred edges. Different silks produce different effects, so experiment and be prepared for some surprises.

---- **YOU WILL NEED** ----

Frame, 45 x 150cm
  (18 x 60in)
Silk habotai
Three-point pins
Gutta, gutta bottle and nib
Paints or dyes: violety red,
  orangey yellow, violety blue
Round brush, No. 12
Foam brush, 5cm (2in)

1. Measure and cut the silk. Place the silk on top of your frame with the right side (the smoothest side) uppermost. Pin one long side of the silk on to the frame, spacing the pins approximately 7.5cm (3in) apart. Pull the silk taut as you pin. Work down the opposite side, tensioning and pulling against the pins as you go.

---- **TIP** ----

When measuring and cutting plain weave silk, you can nick the silk with scissors and then tear along the grain of the fabric – in this way you will always get a straight line.

2. Work down the two short sides.

Opposite page
Sunflower scarves

Long and square summery sunflower scarves are painted on silk habotai and crepe georgette. The colours are applied to damp silk to create soft, blended effects.

3. Draw a line of gutta around the edge of the silk, using a gutta bottle with a gutta nib (see page 29) – this will prevent the colour from spreading on to the frame. Squeeze the bottle as you work and press the nib on to the silk. Check your gutta line for breaks by holding it up to the light. When complete, leave to dry naturally or use a hairdryer to speed up the drying process.

TIP

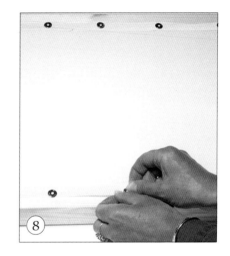

If the gutta nib gets blocked, clear it with a needle.

4. Take the dyes or paints from their bottles using a dropper. Transfer them to a palette.

5. Mix a yellow, red, blue, green and brown (see pages 14–17). Remember that you will not see the true shade of a colour until it is applied to the silk.

6. Pin a spare piece of silk to the edge of the frame and test your colours. Make them a little darker if necessary, as they will dry lighter.

7. Dampen the silk with a foam brush.

8. Dab off any excess water with a piece of paper towelling and adjust the pins if necessary to re-tension the silk.

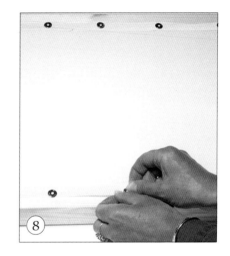

9. Paint the petals yellow, using a No. 12 brush. Always clean your brush in water before applying the next colour.

10. Blend a little red into the base of the yellow petals. If the red is too bright, add water or diffusing medium to dilute it.

11. Paint the centres of the sunflowers brown.

12. Paint the leaves and stems green.

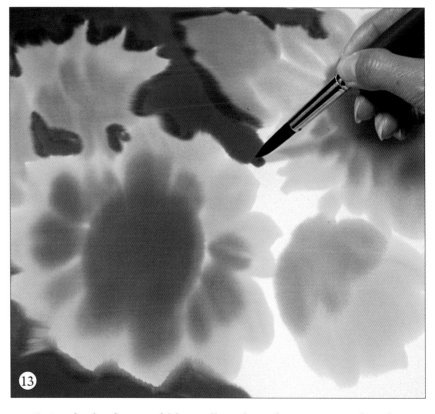

13. Paint the background blue. Allow the colours to spread and blend. Let the silk dry completely, then fix the colours (see pages 58–59).

Mandarin cushion

PAINTING ON DRY SILK

Colours can be painted directly on to dry silk. They tend to spread freely so allow for this when planning your design and leave plenty of white silk around the motifs if you do not want them to merge into each other. You can control the movement of the colour by gently drying with a hairdryer. If you are working with dyes, attractive ragged edges will form around the motifs as the background spreads on to them. To achieve sharp, defined edges, ensure that each application of colour is completely dry before painting the next.

For this project, you can repeat the design on the back of the cushion, or you can use plain blue or orange silk painted to match. For extra strength, line silk cushion covers with cotton lawn.

YOU WILL NEED

Frame, 45cm (18in) square
Silk habotai
Three-point pins
Gutta, gutta bottle and nib
Paints or dyes: violety blue, greeny blue, orangey red, orangey yellow
Round brushes, No. 7 and 12
Hairdryer

1. Apply a line of gutta around the edge of the silk (see page 20). Paint the border, leaves and stalks turquoise using a No. 12 brush.

2. Paint the border and the mandarins orange. Allow to dry completely.

3. Paint in the dark blue background. Work quickly and keep the running edge wet. If right-handed, work from top left to bottom right, and if you are left-handed, from top right to bottom left. When painting around the motifs, do not paint right up to them as the colour will spread. Allow to dry.

4. Use a No. 7 brush to paint in the leaf veins and the dots on the mandarins. Stop the spread of colour immediately by drying it with a hairdryer. When dry, fix the colours (see pages 58–59).

TIP

If the silk wrinkles as you work, re-tension it and add more pins if necessary.

22

Mandarin cushion and scarf
Strong, bold colours are used on this silk habotai cushion and long scarf. They are painted on to dry silk to create ragged edges around the motifs.

Textured effects

USING SALT

Salt is often used in silk painting to produce beautiful random patterns and textures. Different types of salt produce different effects. Fine cooking and table salt create delicate speckled and 'pulled' patterns; coarse rock salt creates larger, mottled and streaking patterns. Effect salt (purchased from silk painting suppliers) has even-sized crystals and can also be used, as can sugar; the latter will produce softer effects.

Using salt is an exciting technique which produces fascinating results. The effects created are surprising and unpredictable and will depend on the dampness of the silk; the tension at which it is stretched; how long the salt is left on for; whether you are using the salt on paint or dye; which colours are used; and how concentrated or diluted the colours are.

The salt crystals are sprinkled on to the painted silk while the paints or dyes are still damp, and the crystals absorb moisture and move the colorants around. The salt effect will not work once the paints or dyes have dried on the silk, but neither should the silk be swimming with colour or the grains of salt will become saturated and so unable to absorb enough moisture to move the colours.

The salt should either be allowed to dry naturally on the silk, or it may be dried gently with a hairdryer. If using a hairdryer, do not hold it too near or you will scatter the damp salt crystals all over your work and speckle it with colour. When the salt is completely dry, brush it off.

Coarse rock salt

Effect salt

24

Fine table salt

Salt left on for different lengths of time

USING RESISTS

Resists block the fibres of the silk. They are used to make barriers which contain the spread of the paints and dyes, and to mask areas of painted or plain silk to prevent subsequent colour washes from penetrating the silk. They are applied in fine lines, or brushed, sponged, splattered or printed on to the silk to create lively marks and textures.

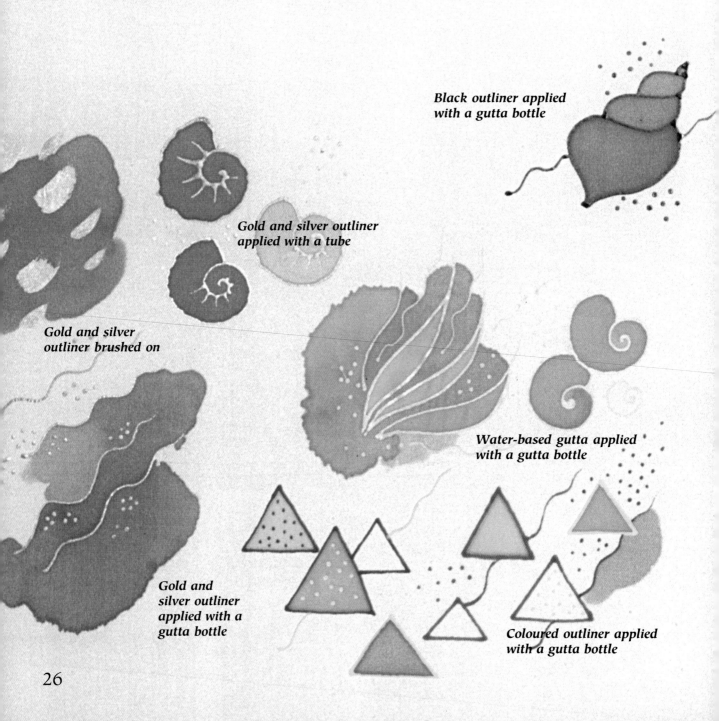

Black outliner applied with a gutta bottle

Gold and silver outliner applied with a tube

Gold and silver outliner brushed on

Water-based gutta applied with a gutta bottle

Gold and silver outliner applied with a gutta bottle

Coloured outliner applied with a gutta bottle

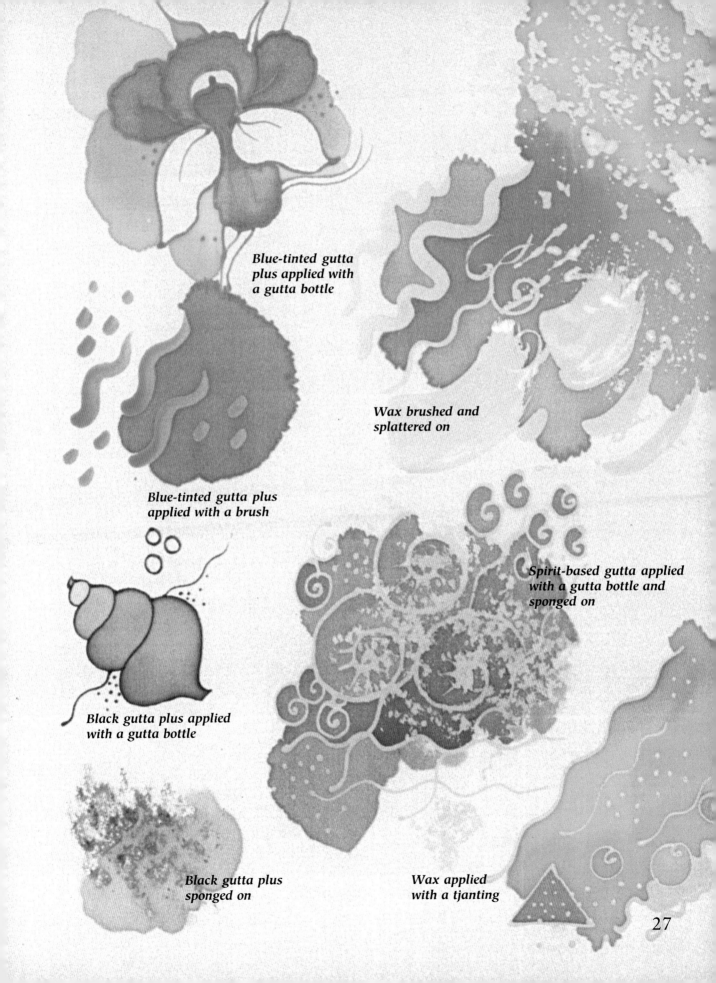

Blue-tinted gutta
plus applied with
a gutta bottle

Wax brushed and
splattered on

Blue-tinted gutta plus
applied with a brush

Spirit-based gutta applied
with a gutta bottle and
sponged on

Black gutta plus applied
with a gutta bottle

Black gutta plus
sponged on

Wax applied
with a tjanting

Iris picture

USING GUTTA

Gutta forms a barrier on the silk and it is the most popular resist used in silk painting. Water-based gutta is easier to use than spirit-based gutta as it can be washed out of the silk after the colours have been fixed, and it may also be stored in the gutta bottle after use. If applied carefully, and if you paint up to it rather than over it, water-based gutta will give very good results. It will, however, stain if painted over and it can also break down if the silk is saturated with water or paint for any length of time. Spirit-based gutta is an excellent resist, but it must be removed from the silk with white spirit or by dry-cleaning.

YOU WILL NEED

Frame, 42.5 x 28.5cm
 (17 x 11¼in)
Silk habotai
Three-point pins
Gutta, gutta bottle and nib
**Paints or dyes: violety blue,
 greeny blue, violety red,
 orangey yellow**
Round brush, No. 7
3B pencil or autofade marker

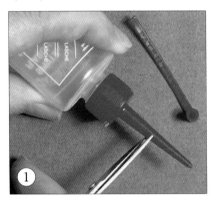

1. Snip off the stopper and half of the spout.

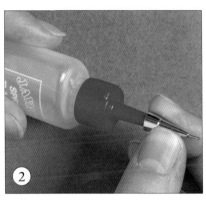

2. Screw on the nib.

TIP

Store gutta bottles of spirit-based gutta in a jam jar with a little white spirit at the bottom to prevent the gutta evaporating and thickening.

Gutta takes about half an hour to dry naturally. If you use a hairdryer, it will take only a few minutes. Test with the tip of your finger; if it is still tacky, dry further.

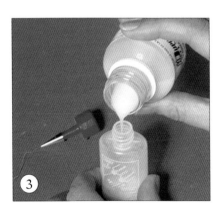

3. Pour the gutta into the gutta bottle.

Opposite

Iris picture and scarf

Delicately shaded irises are painted on to a silk habotai picture, and a crepe georgette scarf. The flowers and leaves are drawn with gutta which contains the spreading colours, and the sunset background is achieved by blending damp colours into each other on the silk.

4. Apply a line of gutta around the edge of the silk (see page 20). Photocopy the pattern, enlarging it by 250%. Place the photocopy underneath the framed silk and support it with a few books or a thick piece of board so that the pattern touches the silk.

5. Trace the design on to the silk using a 3B pencil or an autofade marker. Remove the design and support.

The design for the iris picture   Enlarge by 250% for a full-size pattern

6. Apply gutta over the pencil lines. Hold the bottle at an angle of 45° for line work and vertically for applying the dots. Make a continuous unbroken line for each section, and ensure that there are no gaps where lines join. Leave to dry naturally or dry with a hairdryer.

TIP

Autofade marker fades automatically within a few hours. It also disappears if it comes into contact with water or colorants. Pencil lines will not wash out, so keep them very light.

7. Mix two shades of blue then paint in the flowers with a No. 7 brush.

8. Paint the flower centres yellow as you work.

9. Paint the leaves green.

10. Paint in a blended background (see page 36) by applying yellow and then, whilst still wet, blending pink into it to make orange.

11. Blend blue into the pink to make violet. Leave to dry and then fix the colours (see pages 58–59). Wash out the gutta. Towel-dry the silk and iron it damp.

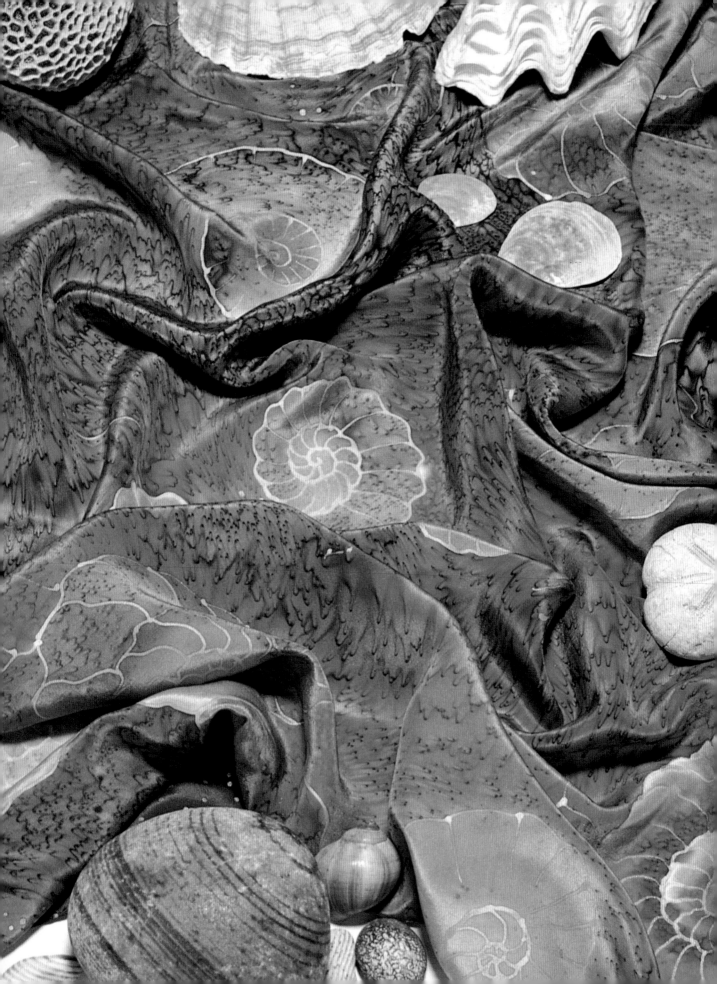

Fossil scarf

USING OUTLINER

Outliner is available in jars and tubes, in black, pearlised and plain colours and in a variety of metallic shades. It is applied to the silk either straight from the tube or it is poured from the jar into a gutta bottle fitted with a gutta nib. Outliner is usually heat-fixed by ironing, but you should always check the manufacturer's instructions.

Outliner remains in the silk after washing which means that it can be felt when the silk is rubbed between the fingers; providing it is not applied too thickly, this is not usually a problem. Metallic outliner (gold, silver and bronze, for example) adds an extra decorative element to a piece of painted silk.

To heat-fix outliner, iron the silk on the wrong side – this will prevent the iron from sticking to the outliner. If used with steam-fix dyes, the outliner should be iron-fixed before steaming. Some outliner, particularly the metallic shades, should not be dry-cleaned. Again, check the instructions on the jar or tube.

> **YOU WILL NEED**
>
> **Frame, 70cm (28in) square**
> **Silk crepe de chine**
> **Three-point pins**
> **Gutta, gutta bottle and nib**
> **Paints or dyes: violety blue, greeny blue, orangey yellow, orangey red**
> **Round brush, No. 12**
> **Foam brush, 2.5cm (1in)**
> **Gold outliner**
> **3B pencil or autofade marker**
> **Table salt**

Fossil scarf

This crepe de chine scarf is painted in soft, muted colours. The fossils are outlined with gold, and the dye is textured with salt crystals to create intriguing swirling patterns.

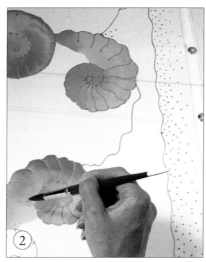

1. Apply a line of gutta around the edge of the silk (see page 20). Trace the fossil design several times on to the silk (see page 30). You can vary the size of the fossil by reducing or enlarging it on a photocopier if you wish. Apply gold outliner to cover all the pencil lines and join some of the fossils with wavy lines to break up the background area. Draw in a border and fill it with dots.

2. Paint in a few fossils using pale blue, pink and yellow. Blend the colours as you work (see page 36).

3. Paint in the blue background between the fossils already worked.

TIP

If you are right-handed, work from the top left to the bottom right to prevent the outliner from smudging. Work from the top right to the bottom left if you are left-handed.

If you are working on a big frame, turn the frame round as you complete each corner.

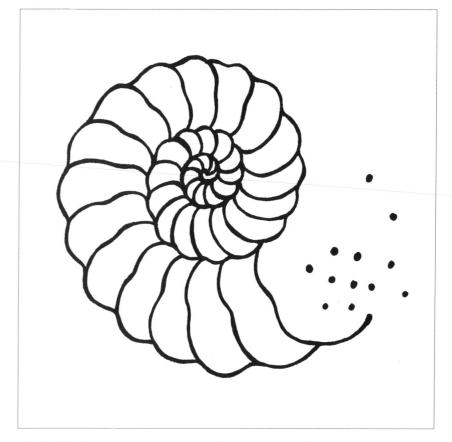

The fossil design   *This pattern can be reduced or enlarged on a photocopier or traced directly on to the silk.*

34

TIP

You can use a hairdryer to halt the effect of the salt. It must be used carefully and from a distance, so it does not scatter the salt grains.

Be careful not to get salt into your dye or paint pots as it will contaminate them.

4. Apply table salt to the painted sections whilst they are still damp. Then, working in small sections, continue painting and sprinkling salt until the design is filled in.

6. Check that there are no grains of salt left on the silk before painting in a dark blue border with a foam brush. Leave to dry and then fix the colours (see pages 58–59).

5. When the salt is completely dry, brush it off with your hands or use a small brush.

Autumn leaves

USING GUTTA WITH A BLENDED WASH

Clear gutta can be applied over pre-painted silk; the silk can then be overpainted and fixed. When the gutta is washed out it leaves either the tinted background colour or no visible line at all – making it an effective technique if you want to avoid white lines in your design.

This project uses gutta applied over a blended background. Effect salt is used to texture the final wash of colour, but the project will work with any type of salt. The scatter of leaves makes a simple design – you can either draw your own, or collect real ones and arrange them in a random pattern before drawing around them.

YOU WILL NEED

Frame, 45 x 150cm (18 x 60in)
Silk habotai
Three-point pins
Gutta, gutta bottle and nib
Paints or dyes: violety red,
  violety blue, orangey yellow
Round brush, No. 12
Salt

---

1. Apply a line of gutta around the edge of the silk (see page 20). Paint on the yellow. While still damp, paint on the pink next to it. Briskly blend across the line where the two colours join using a clean, dry brush. Paint in a line of blue next to the pink and blend. Repeat across the silk. Leave to dry.

2. Outline the design with gutta. You can draw around real leaves if you wish. Leave to dry.

3. Paint the background violet.

4. Sprinkle salt over the background whilst still wet. Flick any grains off the resist lines to prevent the grains transferring colour across into the leaves. Leave to dry before brushing off the salt. Fix the colours (see page 58–59).

Sea spray scarf

USING WAX

Wax may be purchased in blocks, granules or beads and with varying proportions of paraffin wax, beeswax and micro-crystalline waxes. The beginner would be advised to purchase a good general purpose batik wax, either in granules or blocks, which is suitable for use with a tjanting, and will also 'crackle' when cool to create the typical veining associated with batik

It is important to heat the wax to the correct temperature in either a proper wax pot or a double saucepan. If wax is overheated it smokes and can ignite, so care must always be taken to use appropriate equipment and not to leave heating wax unattended. You should also make sure your wax pot or saucepan is stable, and that electric leads cannot be easily pulled and so cause dangerous spills. Keep water away from hot wax and remember that melted wax can burn if splashed on to skin.

Tjantings are the traditional copper- or brass-bowled applicators for hot wax. Brushes and sponges can also be used, but these have a limited life if used for wax – do not, therefore, use your best ones! Old natural-haired and inexpensive Chinese brushes are best; synthetic-haired brushes will shrivel up and become useless. Wax will harden on brushes after use, but it will melt down again next time the brushes are used. Do not leave brushes standing in hot wax, and wipe them off carefully with paper towelling after use.

For this project, silk dyes work best, as paints can spoil the handle of crepe georgette. However, paints can be used if well-diluted.

YOU WILL NEED

Frame, 45 x 180cm (18 x 72in)

Crepe georgette silk

Three-point pins

Gutta, gutta bottle and nib

Paints or dyes: violety blue, greeny blue

Wax

Wax pot or double saucepan

Large coarse-bristled brush

Foam brush, 2.5cm (1in)

Rubber gloves

Iron and ironing board

Old newspapers

Sea spray scarf

This dramatic design on crepe georgette is easy to paint. The waxed areas and blended shades of blue give the impression of breaking waves.

1. Apply a line of gutta around the edge of the silk (see page 20). Apply a little wax to a piece of spare silk to test it. If it is too hot, it will bubble on the silk; if it is too cool, it will turn white. The wax should be dark and transparent as it goes on, and it should penetrate right through to the back of the silk.

2. Brush on the wax in swirls. A colour has been put underneath the silk to make the wax visible for this stage, but it is advisable to work on a plain surface as dark backgrounds can distort the colours of the paints or dyes.

3. Flick and splatter the wax around the swirls.

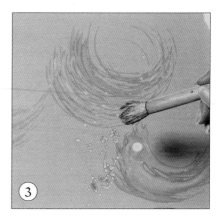

4. Paint straight over the wax using a dark blue and turquoise. As this is a large area, use a 2.5cm (1in) foam brush. Dilute the dark blue as you work if you want a lighter shade.

40

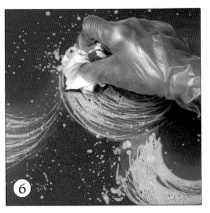

6. Wipe off any surplus blue colour from the surface of the wax with paper towelling. If you have used dyes, wear rubber gloves when doing this, to prevent your hands staining. Leave to dry.

5. Blend the dark blue and turquoise as you work, using a 2.5cm (1in) foam brush.

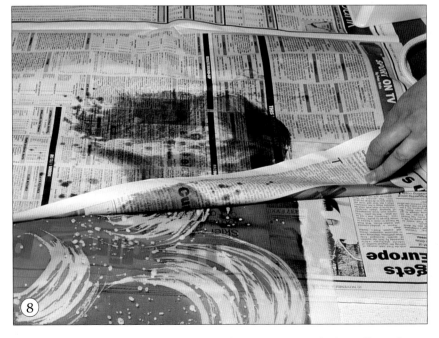

7. Place at least ten sheets of old newspaper on an ironing board. Place the silk on top, and one sheet of newspaper on top of that. Iron over the newspaper with a hot iron until the wax melts and is absorbed by the newspaper.

8. Remove one sheet of newspaper from underneath the silk and replace the top sheet with a clean piece. Continue ironing and removing and replacing the newspaper until it stops absorbing wax. Now move the silk up and do the next section. If you have used dyes, steam fix the colours (see pages 58–59).

Kingfisher cushion
USING WAX

Traditional batik is a dip-dyeing method of patterning fabric using hot wax as a resist. This project uses some batik techniques (although it does not involve using dye baths) combined with silk painting methods. Wax is cracked on the silk so that dye painted over it penetrates to form fine criss-crossing veins typical of batik. A tjanting tool is also used; this allows the hot wax to flow from a fine spout so that lines and dots of wax may be applied. It takes a little practise to use a tjanting, so experiment on a spare piece of silk before beginning the project.

The design for the kingfisher cushion
Enlarge by 400% for a full-size pattern

<table>
<tr><td colspan="2">YOU WILL NEED</td></tr>
</table>

YOU WILL NEED

Frame, 45cm (18in) square
Silk habotai
Three-point pins
Gutta, gutta bottle and nib
Paints or dyes: greeny blue, orangey red, orangey yellow
Batik wax
Wax pot or double saucepan
Tjanting
Round brush, No. 7 and large wide brush
Foam brush, 2.5cm (1in)
3B pencil or autofade marker
Rubber gloves
Iron and ironing board
Old newspapers

Opposite

Kingfisher cushion and scarves

This design captures the brilliant flash of a kingfisher moving across dark water. The cushion is painted on medium-weight habotai and the scarves on light-weight habotai, using wax resist and batik techniques to create a veined effect.

1. Apply a line of gutta around the edge of the silk (see page 20). Photocopy the pattern on page 43, enlarging it by 400%, then trace it on to the silk (see page 30). Heat up some wax, then dip the tjanting into it. Wipe the base of the tjanting with paper towelling.

2. Block the spout of the tjanting with paper towelling to prevent the wax from dripping as you move the tjanting from the wax pot to the silk.

3. Hold the tjanting at an angle, then press the spout on to the silk and draw around the pencil lines. Use a vertical movement when applying the dots.

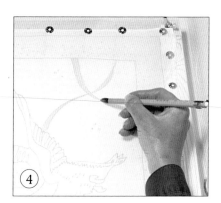

4. Apply the grasses with a No. 7 brush.

TIP

If wax accidentally drips on to your design, add some more to make it look as if they are supposed to be there.

If the spout of the tjanting gets blocked, clear it carefully with a fine needle.

5. Paint in the kingfisher using turquoise, yellow and orange.

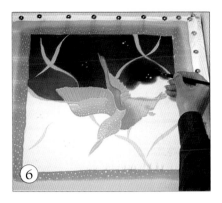

6. Paint the border yellow and orange, and the background blue. Allow to dry thoroughly.

7. Paint over the silk with wax, using a large, wide brush. Make sure you cover the silk completely. Allow to cool.

8. Take the silk off the frame then scrunch it up.

9. Roughly re-pin the silk, then paint over it with dark blue using a 2.5cm (1in) foam brush. Wipe off the surplus colour (see page 41). When dry, iron between newspaper to remove the wax (see page 41). If you have used dyes, steam fix the colours (see pages 58–59).

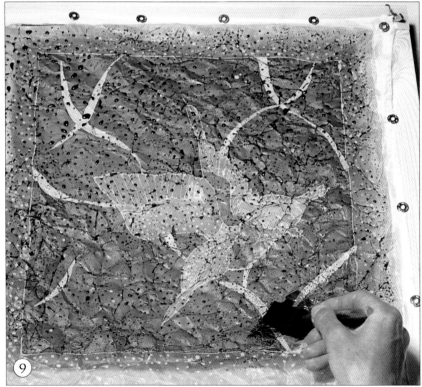

45

MOVING ON

Many exciting and unique effects can be achieved in silk painting. As silk paints and dyes are semi-transparent and transparent, beautiful results can be created by overpainting and building them up. Colours can be blended, gradated and shaded into each other while they are still damp; special effects can be produced by painting on to silk treated with salt solution or anti-spread medium; discharge paste can be used to remove dye; and diffusing medium can be used to disperse and pattern areas painted with dye. Some of these techniques work well with iron-fix paints (such as painting on salt solution) and some will only work with steam-fix dyes. Check the list of materials given at the beginning of each project before you begin, to see whether paints or dyes are specified.

Spots of diluted dye left to spread on dry, blended dyes

Colours blended and shaded

Spots of diluted dye painted twice on dry, blended dyes

Paints applied on top of salt solution

Dyes dispersed with diffusing medium

Discharge paste applied with a gutta bottle

Discharge paste applied with a brush

Discharge paste sponged on

Spots and lines of diffusing medium painted on to dry, blended dyes

Spots and lines of diluted dye dried quickly with a hairdryer

Paints and dyes brushed on to silk treated with anti-spread

Dyes blended into diffusing medium

Paints and dyes sponged on to silk treated with anti-spread

Velvet cushion

USING DISCHARGE PASTE

Painted silk velvet is rich and sumptuous, but you need to mix plenty of colour as the velvet absorbs a great deal. Use steam-fix dyes rather than iron-fix paints, as the latter will spoil the pile of the fabric. For this project, you could paint a matching back for the cushion, and to give a really regal look you could edge the cushion with piping and tassels.

1. Loop stenter pins around the frame and through the elastic bands. Hook the pins on to the edge of the velvet.

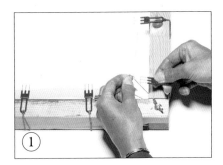

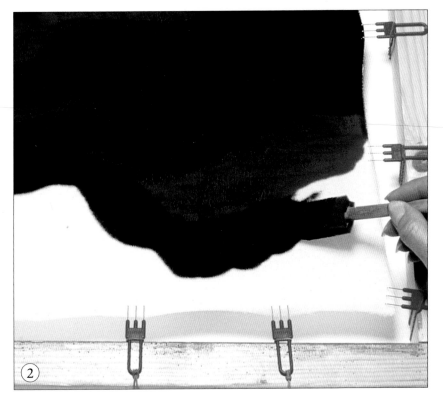

TIP

Gutta will not penetrate velvet as the fabric is too thick. Use stenter pins instead of a line of gutta to prevent the frame getting messy.

You can use discharge paste with other silks, either sponged or brushed on. It will not always produce white, but it will discharge out to paler colours. The effect is only seen when the silk is fixed.

After fixing and washing out discharge paste, you can paint contrasting colours into the discharged areas. Make sure that the silk is dry before you start, and remember to re-fix the colours

2. Mix up your dyes and then paint on irregular stripes of red, orange, blue and purple using a foam brush. Blend the colours as you go. It is best to use a different brush for each colour. Leave to dry.

3. Lightly sponge the velvet with discharge paste to create random mottling. Protect your hands by wearing rubber gloves. When dry, steam-fix the velvet (see pages 48–49). If you are steam-fixing yourself, use thick cotton cloth. Wash out surplus dye under cold running water then spin dry for thirty seconds. Tumble dry on a low setting for ten to twenty minutes. For extra sheen, iron in the direction of the pile whilst still damp.

Velvet scarf and cushions

Silk velvet scarves and cushions look wonderfully rich and sumptuous as the colours catch the light. You can trim the edges of cushions with piping and tassels for a really regal look, and scarves and stoles look beautiful backed with silk satin.

Striped scarf

USING DIFFUSING MEDIUM

Diffusing medium is a clear liquid supplied under a variety of names and it is available in either a concentrated or ready-mixed form. It helps dyes to spread and blend evenly and is very useful if you are painting large areas of colour. Diffusing medium can also be used instead of water to dilute the dyes and obtain pastel tints. Delicate tonal gradations can be created on the silk by blending dyes into areas painted with diffusing medium and it may also be used to mottle and pattern the painted silk. When it is applied to dry, dyed areas it disperses the colour to form lighter patches, often with a darker edge. Experiment by applying stripes, spots and wavy lines to a piece of silk painted with dyes. This project uses stripes of diffusing medium to disperse the colour, and the spread of the stripes is controlled with a hairdryer.

YOU WILL NEED

Frame, 45 x 180cm (18 x 72in)

Silk crepe georgette

Three-point pins

Gutta, gutta bottle and nib

Steam-fix dyes: violety blue, orangey red, orangey yellow

Round brush, No. 12

Foam brush, 2.5cm (1in)

Diffusing medium

Hairdryer

1. Apply a line of gutta around the edge of the silk (see page 20). Mix your colours. Apply a stripe of burgundy and then violet using a foam brush.

2. Work quickly with a clean, dryish No. 12 brush to blend the two colours smoothly together.

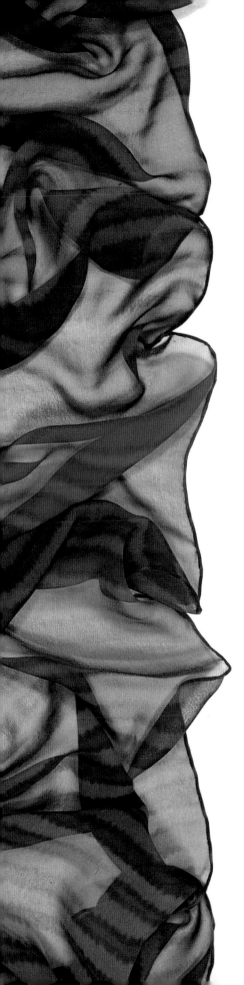

3. Continue adding stripes of colours and blending them as you work. Allow the silk to dry naturally.

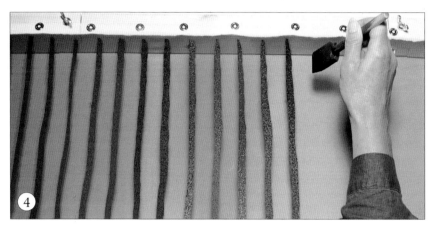

4. Paint on fine lines of diffusing medium using the narrow edge of a foam brush. Continue until the silk is covered with smooth, even stripes.

5. Allow the diffusing medium to spread slightly and then halt the spread by drying the lines with a hairdryer. Steam fix (see pages 58–59).

Striped scarf

This sophisticated crepe georgette scarf is easy to paint using a blended wash of dyes; diffusing medium creates the striped effect. Choose your own colours to coordinate with any outfit.

Exotic orchid wallhanging

USING DYE-TINTED GUTTA

A special thick gutta, usually called gutta plus, is used with steam-fix dyes to create a dyed resist line. The gutta itself is washed out of the silk after fixing, leaving the dye-stained line. As outliner is left in the silk and can be felt, it can spoil the drape of the cloth, so gutta plus is often a better alternative if you are working with steam-fix dyes. By tinting your own gutta, the linear element of your painting can be unified with the other colours in your design.

YOU WILL NEED

Frame, 45 x 30cm (18 x 12in)
Silk habotai
Three-point pins
Gutta, gutta bottle and nib
Steam-fix dyes: violety blue, greeny blue, greeny yellow, orangey red
Gutta plus
Diffusing medium
Round brush, No. 7
3B pencil or autofade marker
Teaspoon

TIP

Gutta plus is available uncoloured, so you can add your own dye to colour it to the required shade. If you add too much dye, the gutta will spread and it will not resist.

Exotic orchid wallhanging

Dye-tinted gutta is used to create the turquoise lines in this vibrant wallhanging on silk habotai, and diffusing medium and diluted violet dye are painted over a greeny-gold to pattern the background.

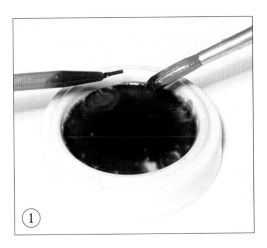

1. Apply a line of gutta around the edge of the silk (see page 20). Add a few drops of turquoise dye to a small amount of gutta plus and mix with a brush. Transfer into a gutta bottle with a teaspoon.

2. Photocopy the pattern, enlarging it by 300%, then trace it on to the silk (see page 30). Cover the lines of the design with dye-tinted gutta. Allow to dry.

3. Paint in the orchids using blue, turquoise, green and violet. Blend the colours to create variations in tone. Use greeny-gold for the background. When the colour is dry, pattern the background using diffusing medium and diluted violet dye. Steam-fix the colours, then rinse out the gutta to leave the dye-stained line.

The design for the exotic orchid wallhanging
Enlarge by 300% for a full-size pattern

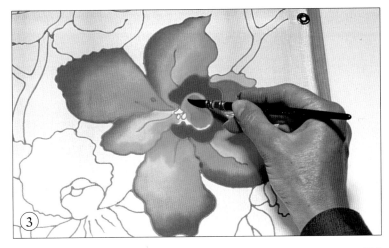

Greek mountain landscape
This delicate landscape was inspired by a visit to Corfu. The white speckles are formed by painting on to silk treated with salt solution. The salt crystallises and makes little dots, giving the finished painting a pointillist look.

Greek mountain landscape

USING SALT SOLUTION

Salt can be used in solution to treat the silk prior to painting. Striking coral-like effects are achieved by applying the paints and dyes over the dried, crystallised solution. This technique works best with iron-fix paints. You can use steam-fix dyes but you will not get the same pronounced white speckling.

1. Apply a line of gutta around the edge of the silk (see page 20). Add a tablespoon of rock or sea salt to 100ml (3½ fl oz) of hot water. Stir until completely dissolved.

TIP
For larger crystals and bigger dots, paint on a second coat of salt solution once the first has dried.

YOU WILL NEED
Frame, 45 x 30cm (18 x 12in)
Silk habotai
Three-point pins
Gutta, gutta bottle and nib
Paints or dyes: greeny blue, violety blue, greeny yellow, violety yellow
Rock or sea salt
Foam brush 2.5cm (1in)
Round brushes, No. 7 and 12
Beaker
Tablespoon

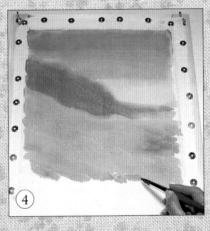

2. Paint the salt solution on to the silk using a foam brush. Leave it to dry slowly in a cool room. Do not use a hairdryer to speed up the drying process. When completely dry, crystals will have formed, dotting the surface of the silk.

3. Paint in the sky, working from a dark to a light blue. Use a blue-violet for the distant mountain range, and different shades of green for the hills and fields. Leave a plain area of silk for the house.

4. Paint in the orange roof of the house. Leave to dry before adding the trees in the foreground. Fix the colours (see pages 58–59) before washing the salt out.

Flower and grape panel

USING ANTI-SPREAD

Anti-spread is a clear or milky liquid, slightly thicker than diffusing medium. It is used to treat silk prior to painting to prevent the dyes or paints from spreading. The silk is transformed into a paper-like surface which can then be painted freely, stencilled, sponged and so on without the need for resists. It can be painted all over the silk or in selected areas so that contrasts of free-spreading and controlled colour are achieved. Anti-spread should be applied thinly and evenly and it should be dried thoroughly before painting.

For this project, if you do not have the confidence to paint freely on to the silk, use an autofade marker and sketch out the design first.

1. Apply a line of gutta around the edge of the silk (see page 20). Apply anti-spread on to the silk smoothly and evenly using a foam brush. Leave to dry.

2. Paint in the design. Do not overload the colour on your brush as this can result in fuzzy lines. Blend colours as you work and use darker tones to add depth. Fix the colours (see pages 58–59) then rinse out the anti-spread with warm water.

Flower panel

This decorative panel is painted on to silk habotai treated with anti-spread solution. The highlights on the grapes and the edges of the flowers and leaves have been left white to make the design more striking.

Finishing off

ADDING DETAIL

Details can be added to silk paintings in various ways. One technique is to mix the paint or dye with thickener to stop it spreading, and to then apply it with a brush, or to print, stencil or sponge it on to the silk. The thickener is washed out after fixing. Metallic outliner can also be brushed, sponged or printed on to the silk to give an ornate finish. Iron-fix fabric felt-tips can be drawn or stippled on to add fine details; if you use these with dyes, iron-fix them before steaming.

Clockwise*: gold outliner applied with a brush; iron-fix fabric felt-tips; dye mixed with thickener.*

GLOSSARY

Anti-spread medium

This is also known as *anti-fusant*, *malgrund* or primer. It is a clear or milky liquid which is used to treat the silk to prevent the dyes or paints from spreading so that watercolour effects can be achieved. It is washed out of the silk after fixing.

Autofade marker

This is used to draw on to the silk. The line fades within a few hours or disappears as soon as water or colours are applied.

Diffusing medium

Also known as thinner or *diluant*. It can be mixed with the dyes instead of water to make them spread more evenly and to produce pastel tints. It may also be used to disperse and mottle areas of dyed silk.

Discharge paste

A bleaching agent used to remove areas painted with steam-fix dyes. It can be sponged, brushed or printed on, or applied with a gutta bottle.

Fixing

A technique which makes painted silk light-fast, washable and dry-cleanable.

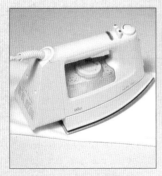

Silk paints are fixed by ironing

Silk dyes are fixed by steaming

Iron fixing

Unlike silk dyes which are fixed by steaming, acrylic-based silk paints are fixed by ironing. Before you start, protect your ironing board with a piece of cotton cloth.

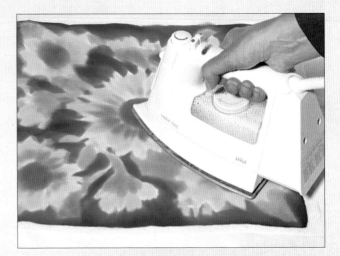

Use a dry iron without steam and adjust it to the cotton setting. Iron evenly on the reverse side of the silk for about two to three minutes. If you have used outliner or gutta in your silk, cover the silk with a thin cloth to prevent the iron from sticking.

Steam fixing

Silk dyes are fixed by steaming. Steaming times vary depending on the type of silk used and the quantity being steamed. Some firms and individual silk painters offer a steaming service – check with your local supplier or mail order company. Large pieces of silk must be steamed in a professional steamer, but it is possible to steam pieces up to one metre square in a domestic pressure-cooker or a vegetable steamer at home – it is important that these items are reserved for silk painting only. It is well worth mastering the steam-fixing method as dyes do produce an excellent quality of colour and finish. Steam-fixing is not difficult, but the procedure must be followed precisely to avoid disappointment. Practise on pieces that are not too precious to begin with!

TIP

Make sure hands, cotton and the work surface are all completely dry before you begin steam-fixing as any drops of water will mark the silk.

1. Cut out a piece of clean, dry cloth (thin cotton sheeting is ideal) approximately 10cm (4in) bigger all round than the piece of silk that you want to steam. Lay the silk flat in the middle of the cloth and smooth out any creases. Roll up the cloth and silk loosely.

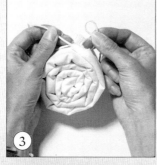

2. Coil the roll to make a snail.

3. Secure the bundle with string. Tuck in loose ends of string to make a neat package.

4. Cut four circles of foil to fit inside the steamer. Place two circles in the bottom of the steamer, put the bundle on top, and then place the remaining two circles of foil on top of the bundle. Smooth down the foil over the sides of the bundle to make an umbrella shape – this will prevent condensation from dripping on to the bundle.

5. Fill a saucepan one third full of boiling water. Place the lid on the steamer then place the steamer on top of the saucepan. Steam for one to two hours depending on the size of the silk (if you use a pressure cooker, twenty minutes should be sufficient). If you are using a saucepan and have to top up the water level during this time, use boiling water. When the silk is steamed, unwrap it and rinse it in cold running water to remove any dye residue. Towel dry and iron damp on a cotton/silk setting to remove creases.

TIP

The main problem with steaming is water getting into contact with the bundle – either because the bundle is too large and touches the sides of the steamer, or the foil is too small and condensation drips. Use new foil as old pieces can have tiny holes in, which will allow moisture to drip through. The foil should be a minimum of an inch larger all round than the bundle to prevent condensation from dripping on to the bundle.

Do not put too much water in the saucepan or it may splash up into your bundle of silk.

Frames

The silk is pinned to a wooden frame so that it does not touch the table surface while it is being painted. Because the silk is suspended, the resist can be applied right through to the underneath of the silk without it sticking to or smearing on the table. The paints and dyes can also spread freely and can dry without marking. Drawing pins, three-point pins or stenter pins can be used to attach the silk to the frame. Always use a frame large enough for the piece of silk to be painted. Pin-holes and joins in the painting can show if you have to move the silk up.

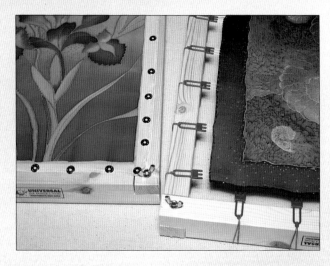

Simple fixed frame
This can be made with 3.5 x 4.5cm (1½ x 1¾in) timber jointed and screwed at the corners or simply fixed at the corners with metal brackets.

Home-made frame
This can be made using an old drawer or a picture frame.

Adjustable frame
This can be made or bought from silk painting suppliers. It is suitable for painting different sizes of silk. Different sorts are available with slotted sides which fit into each other at intervals, sliding grooves with bolts and wing nuts, or sections which bolt together.

Gutta

A resist.

Spirit-based gutta
A clear, liquid rubber which is thinned with white spirit to obtain the consistency of liquid honey. It forms a very effective barrier on the silk as it is completely water-repellent. It is removed from the silk by dry-cleaning or with white spirit or gutta solvent.

Water-based gutta
A synthetic substitute to spirit-based gutta. It is removed by washing. It does not form quite such an effective resist as spirit-based gutta but tends to be more popular as it is so easy to remove.

Gutta plus
This is a thick, water-based gutta which is tinted with steam-fix dyes. It is rinsed out of the silk after steaming to leave a dyed line.

Gutta bottle

A small plastic bottle with a screw-top and a spouted lid. It is used as a resist applicator. The plastic spout produces a crude resist line, so it is better to snip it off and fit a gutta nib.

Gutta nib

Sometimes called a 'normographic pen'. A little metal spout which can be screwed or pushed on to the plastic spout of the gutta bottle. The nib is supplied with a piece of fine fuse wire. A gutta bottle should be stored with this wire pushed into the nozzle of the gutta nib to prevent it drying out. Do not use the wire to unblock the nib – use a fine needle instead.

Outliner

A resist. Available in black, pearlised and plain colours and a variety of metallic shades. It is iron-fixable and remains in the silk after washing.

Pins

Used to attach and stretch the silk on to the frame.

Three-point silk pins
These are sharp, will not snag the silk and are easy to push in and to remove. Drawing pins can also be used but are harder to push into the wood and they can damage the silk.

Stenter pins

Stenter pins

These are useful for silk with pre-rolled edges, or small or awkward shaped items such as ties. They have three long prongs bent at right-angles and set into a plastic mount. They are attached to the frame with elastic bands, either pinned on to the frame with the flat pins, or looped around it.

Resist

A substance which blocks the fibres of the silk and prevents the paints or dyes from penetrating the fabric. In silk painting, resists are usually applied as a fine line which forms a barrier across which the paints and dyes cannot spread. Resist lines are used to separate areas of different colours and create linear definition in painting.

Rolled edges

Painted scarves look better with rolled edges. You can buy a range of different sizes and types of silk scarves ready for painting which come with pre-rolled edges, or you can roll your own as shown.

1. Thread up a long fine needle and knot the end. Hold the needle between thumb and forefinger then take the silk in both hands, with the wrong side facing you. Hold the silk carefully between fingers and thumbs and roll the raw edge towards you. Secure the end of the roll with a tiny stitch.

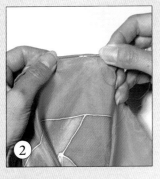

2. Run the needle into the roll of silk, then nick the right side of the silk with a tiny stitch as shown. Run the needle back along the inside of the roll, nick with a stitch and repeat to build up a series of tiny stitches. Place each stitch approximately 1cm (½in) apart. Continue rolling and stitching the silk down the entire edge.

Salt

Used to produce random patterns on silk. It is sprinkled on to wet paint or dye or it is used in solution to treat the silk with prior to painting.

Silks

A number of different types of silk are suitable for painting on. Each silk has its own characteristics in weave and handle. Some silks are heavy and fluid, some are light and floaty. It is a good idea to experiment on a number of different silks to discover the particular qualities of each one. Colours and resists will react differently but as a general rule, the thicker the silk, the more dye is needed to colour it and the more difficult it is to get the resists to penetrate right through it.

TIP

If the dyes or paints sit in beads on the surface of the silk and will not sink in, there is dressing or gum in the silk. You can hand wash the silk with pure soap powder in very hot water to remove the gum. A silk with a heavier dressing may need to be boiled for up to an hour.

Silks are sold by weight, either in grammes per running metre or by the Chinese measurement called a *momme*. You will usually find that the lighter the silk, the cheaper it is. Some of the most popular silks used in silk painting are:

Silk crepe de chine

Crepe de chine is a fluid silk with a beautiful sheen which produces exceptionally rich and vibrant colours when painted with silk dyes. It drapes well and is lovely for scarves, clothing, lined cushions and wallhangings. Choose a No. 9 weight to begin with. The heavier weights absorb a lot of dye and extra care must be taken in applying the resists to ensure complete penetration of the fibre.

Silk crepe georgette

Crepe georgette is a semi-transparent, matt-surfaced silk with a springy quality which makes it excellent for scarves as it does not crease easily. Its rougher texture and transparency make it a little more difficult to work on. It is sometimes difficult to apply the resist smoothly on to crepe georgette (the nib can catch on the elastic surface), breaks in the line cannot be seen so easily as on the denser weaves, and the dyes do not spread as freely. However, it is well worth practising on crepe georgette as it has its own special beauty when painted, especially when used as a draped and folded textile where the overlapping colours show through and build up to create surprising effects and great depth of colour.

Silk gauze chiffon
Gauze chiffon is a very light, transparent, delicate silk with a gossamer, floaty quality. It is beautiful for scarves or layered over less transparent silks in dresses. Care must be taken not to snag it with fingernails or rough-spouted gutta nibs.

Silk habotai or pongee
Pongee is a general term used to describe a soft, plain weave silk of Chinese origin. Silk habotai is often referred to as pongee. Habotai is probably the best choice for beginners. The plain weave and smooth surface makes it ideal for painting on as the resists are easy to apply and the colours spread freely. Choose a habotai No. 5 weight for experimental work and light-weight scarves, and a habotai No. 9 for framed pictures, garments, lined cushions and more substantial scarves.

Silk jacquard
Jacquards have a woven design incorporated into them. Jacquards are interesting to paint on as the design of the weave adds another dimension to the painting. They can be purchased in a number of different patterns such as spots, stripes, florals and abstracts. Different silk types are produced in a jacquard weave, such as crepe satin jacquard, crepe de chine jacquard and douppion jacquard.

Silk satin
Satin is a heavy, fluid silk with a high sheen. It is beautiful for evening wear and makes dramatic scarves. Use steam-fix dyes on it.

Silk twill
Twill has a diagonal weave and is popular for clothing and scarves. It is very soft, easy to paint on and it takes the colour well. The edges of twill scarves may be fringed to give a decorative finish.

Silk paints
These are acrylic-based and are fixed by ironing to make them colour-fast and washable. They are semi-transparent with a milky consistency. They are easy for the beginner to use because of the simple fixing process. Always wash brushes and palettes well as colour is difficult to remove when dry.

Silk dyes
These are fixed by steaming to make them colour-fast and washable. They are transparent, liquid and produce very strong, vibrant colours on silk. They give better results on most silks as they do not alter the sheen or handle of the silk, and they tend to be easier to work with as the dyes can be manipulated more easily than paints – they are therefore more versatile. There are some dyes on the market which require a chemical fixing process; check the manufacturer's instructions carefully.

Thickener or epaississant
A clear or brownish gum which is mixed with the paints or dyes to make them thick so that they can be applied with a brush or screen-printed on to silk. The thickener prevents the colour from spreading.

Tjanting
A brass or copper-bowled Javanese tool with a fine spout (or spouts) used to apply melted wax. It is also sometimes referred to as a canting.

Wax
Hot, melted wax is used as a resist. It may be applied with a tjanting, or it may be brushed, splattered, sponged or printed on to the silk. It is removed by ironing between sheets of old newspaper. If a residue remains, it can be removed after fixing by dry cleaning or with white spirit.

Common mistakes

All silk painters make mistakes, even experienced ones. To help you identify and so resolve problems, here are some of the most common ones to watch out for.

The resist line is smudged

The resist line is too thin

The resist line is too thick

There is a break in the resist line

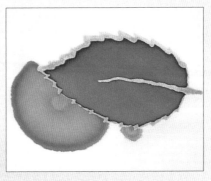

Too much colour is applied and the resist line is flooded

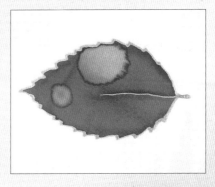

Drops of water are splashed on to silk before colours have been fixed

> ## TIP
>
> **Repair broken resist lines when the colour has dried by redrawing them.**
>
> **Allow gutta or outliner to dry before painting over 'bleeds'.**
>
> **Diffusing medium or dyes can usually be blended over bleeds to reduce them.**
>
> **Bleeds in paints can be difficult to conceal, so adapt them to make them part of your design.**

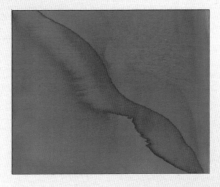

Watermarks and hard edges form because painting is not quick enough; colours have dried unevenly; colours have been dried too quickly with a hairdryer

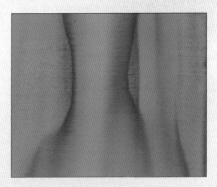

Silk is not stretched tightly enough on the frame

Index

anti-fusant   *see anti-spread medium*
anti-spread medium 8, 10, 46, 47, 56, 58
autofade marker 8, 10, 30, 56, 58,

batik 38, 43
blending 12, 31, 36, 50–51
brush 8, 10, 12, 21, 38

canting   *see tjanting*
colour mixing 14–15, 16
colour wheel 16–17
complementary colours 16–17
cushion
   kingfisher 42–45
   mandarin 22–23
   velvet 48–49

diffusing medium 4, 8, 10, 13, 46, 47,
   50–51, 53, 58
diluant   *see diffusing medium*
discharge paste 46, 47, 48–49, 58
double saucepan 9, 38
dropper 8, 10, 20
dyes 4, 7, 8, 10, 12–13, 20, 33, 38,
   41, 46, 48, 52, 55, 57, 58, 62

epaississant   *see thickener*

felt-tips 57
fixing
   iron 8, 11, 12, 33, 57, 58
   steam 9, 11, 12, 13, 49, 53, 58–59
foam brush 8, 10
frame 9, 11, 60

gutta 8, 10, 20, 26, 27, 29, 30, 31,
   36, 48, 58, 60
   drying 29
   edging silk with 20
gutta bottle 8, 10, 26, 33, 53, 60
gutta nib 8, 10, 20, 33, 60
   fitting a 29
gutta plus 4, 8, 27, 52–53, 60
gutta solvent 60

hairdryer 8, 11, 12, 13, 20, 22, 24,
   29, 35, 50, 51, 55, 63

iron 8, 11, 31, 41, 49, 58, 62

jam jar 8, 11

landscape, Greek mountain 54–55

malgrund   *see anti-spread medium*

newspaper 41

outliner 8, 10, 33, 34, 52, 58, 60
   black 33
   coloured 8, 10, 26
   metallic 8, 10, 26, 33, 34, 57
   pearlised 33

paints 7, 8, 10, 12, 20, 38, 46, 48,
   55, 58, 62
palette 8, 10, 20
panel, flower and grape 56
paper towelling 8, 9, 11, 20, 38, 41, 44
pattern
   exotic orchid wallhanging   53
   fossil 34
   iris picture 30
   kingfisher   43
pencil 8, 10, 30
picture, iris 28–31
pins
   stenter 9, 11, 48, 61
   three-point 9, 11, 60
pinning 19, 22, 63
pongee   *see silk, habotai*
pressure-cooker 58
primer   *see anti-spread medium*

resist 26–27, 43, 52, 60, 61, 63
rolled edge 9, 61
rubber gloves 9, 11, 41, 49

salt 8, 11, 24–25, 33, 35, 36–37, 61
   coarse rock 24, 55
   effect 24
   fine table 24
   sea 55
   solution 46, 54, 55

scarf
   fossil 32–35
   iris 29
   kingfisher 43
   sea spray 38–41
   striped 50–51
   sunflower 18–21
   velvet 49
scissors 8, 19, 10
silk 7, 8, 10, 19, 61
   crepe de chine 33, 61
   crepe georgette 19, 29, 38, 51, 61–62
   gauze chiffon 62
   habotai 4, 19, 23, 29, 43, 52, 56, 62
   jacquard 62
   satin 62
   twill 62
   velvet 48–49
sponge 8, 10, 38
steamer 9, 11, 58, 59
sugar 24

thickener 8, 10, 57, 62
thinner   *see diffusing medium*
tin foil 9, 11, 58, 61
tjanting 9, 11, 27, 38, 43, 44, 62
tracing 30

vegetable steamer   *see steamer*

wallhanging, exotic orchid 52–53
watermark 12, 63
wax 9, 11, 27, 38–41, 43, 44, 45, 62
wax pot 9, 11, 38